The Bed Book

The Bed Book

by Sylvia Plath
Pictures by Emily Arnold McCully

Harper & Row, Publishers
New York, Hagerstown, San Francisco, London

BEDS come in all sizes–
single or double,
cot-size or cradle,
king-size or trundle.

Most Beds are Beds
for sleeping or resting,
but the *best* Beds are much
more interesting!

Not just a white little
tucked-in-tight little
nighty-night little
turn-out-the-light little
     bed–
     instead

a Bed for Fishing,
a Bed for Cats,

a Bed for a Troupe of
Acrobats.

The *right* sort of Bed
(if you see what I mean)
is a Bed that might
be a Submarine
nosing through water
clear and green,
silver and glittery
as a sardine.

Or a Jet-Propelled Bed
for visiting Mars
with mosquito nets
for the shooting stars.

If you get hungry
in the middle of the night
a Snack Bed is good
for the appetite–
with a pillow of bread
to nibble at
and up at the head
an Automat
where you need no shillings,
just a finger to stick in
the slot, and out come
cakes and cold chicken.

Another Bed
that fills the bill
is the sort of Bed
that is Spottable–

in a Spottable Bed
it *never* matters
where jam rambles
and where paint splatters!

Or if the cat
and the parakeet
dance on the covers
with muddyish feet.

On the other hand,
if you want to *move*
a Tank Bed's the Bed
most movers approve.
A Tank Bed's got cranks
and wheels and cogs
and levers to pull
if you're stuck in bogs.
A Tank Bed's treads
go upstairs or down,
through duck ponds or through

a cobbledy town.
And you're snug inside
if it rains or hails.
A Tank Bed's got
everything but sails!

Now a gentler Bed
is a good deal more
the sort of Bed
bird-watchers adore–
a kind of hammock
between two tall trees

where you can swing
in the leaves at ease.
All the birds would flock
(if I'm not mistaken)
to your berries and cherries
and bits of bacon.

None of these Beds,
of course, is very
easy to fold up
or fetch and carry
so a Pocket-size Bed
is a fine Bed to own
when you're eating out
with friend Jim or Aunt Joan
and they say: *It's too bad*
you can't stay overnight
but there isn't an extra
Bed in sight.
You can take out your Bed
shrunk small as a pea

and water it till
it grows suitably.
Yes, a Pocket-size Bed
works very well
only how can you tell,
O how can you tell
it won't shrink back
to the size of a pea
while you're asleep in it?
Then where would you be!

O here is a Bed
shrinkproofer than that
a floatier, boatier
Bed than that!

In an Elephant Bed
you go where you please.
You pick bananas
right out of the trees.

An Elephant Bed
is where kings ride.
It's cool as a pool
in the shade inside.
You can climb up the trunk
and slide down behind.
Everyone knows
elephants don't mind!

And when it's lots
of degrees below
a North-Pole Bed
is the best I know.
A North-Pole Bed
is made of fur.
It's fine if you're
an ex-plor-er,
or if you just
have a very cold nose.
There's a built-in oven
to warm your toes.

O who cares much
if a Bed's big or small
or lumpy and bumpy—
who cares at all
as long as its springs
arc bouncy and new.

From a Bounceable Bed
you bounce into the blue–
over the hollyhocks
(Toodle-oo!)
over the owls'
to-whit-to-whoo,
over the moon
to Timbuktoo
with springier springs
than a kangaroo.

You can see if the Big Dipper's
full of stew,
and you may want to stay
up a week or two.

These are the Beds
for me and for you!
These are the Beds
to climb into:

Pocket-size Beds
and Beds for Snacks,
Tank Beds, Beds
on Elephant Backs,
Beds that fly,
or go under water,
Bouncy Beds, Beds
you can spatter and spotter,
Bird-Watching Beds,
Beds for Zero Weather–
any kind of Bed
as long as it's rather
special and queer
and full of surprises,

Beds of amazing
shapes and sizes–

NOT just a white little
tucked-in-tight little
nighty-night little
turn-out-the-light little
bed!